The
Kindness
Journal

Little Activities to Make
a Big Difference

JAIME THURSTON
Founder of

LOM
ART

First published in Great Britain in 2021 by LOM ART,
an imprint of Michael O'Mara Books Limited
9 Lion Yard
Tremadoc Road
London SW4 7NQ

A CIP catalogue record for this book is available from the British Library.

Papers used by Michael O'Mara Books Limited are natural,
recyclable products made from wood grown in sustainable
forests. The manufacturing processes conform to the
environmental regulations of the country of origin.

ISBN: 978-1-912785-38-4 in paperback print format

1 2 3 4 5 6 7 8 9 10

Illustrated by Nadia Taylor
Designed by Natasha Le Coultre

Printed and bound in China

www.mombooks.com

THE

Kindness
Journal

Dedication

For my mum ... the kindest
person on the planet.

Contents

Introduction

We all need kindness. It helps us feel happy, calm and more connected.

It also determines almost every aspect of our lives ... what kind of relationship we have with ourselves, what kind of home-life we have, how strong our communities are and, ultimately, what kind of world we live in. It really is what matters most.

We might not always feel kind, but there is a
constant source of kindness inside all of us. It can
sometimes be overshadowed by negative thoughts
or lost in our busy minds, but it's always there.

This journal will help you tap into it. It's a place to reflect,
to feel inspired and to realize the positive effect kindness
has, not only on those we are kind to but on our own
physical and mental health. The more we learn about
the science of kindness, the more we understand that
kindness is not a luxury, or simply 'nice to have'. It's
essential – we all need it for our well-being. I hope that
within these pages, you find some time and space to focus
on kindness, even if it's just for a few minutes a day.

The Kindness Journal, will help to raise money and awareness of 52 Lives, the kindness charity. 10% of the author's royalties from the sale of this book will be donated to 52 Lives, a registered charity in England and Wales (charity number 1166238).

52 Lives helps to change someone's life every week with the help of almost 100,000 people. We give people tangible help, but the most important thing we do is spread kindness. We also run a School of Kindness, working with thousands of children every year. We want to help children realize that the little choices they make every day matter, and that they have the power to change the world.

52LIVES

www.52-Lives.org

www.SchoolofKindness.org

Acknowledgements

Thank you to everyone who supports the
52 Lives charity. None of what we do would be
possible without the help of our kind community
of supporters and our corporate partner, Gala
Bingo, who raise funds every single week to
help us change lives and spread kindness.

What does kindness mean to you?

'Be kind' – two words we hear so often, but what does this actually mean?

Is it giving your time? Your money? Is it seeing the good in people? Is it a one-off act or an approach to life? Take a moment to decide what 'being kind' means to you. It can be as big or as small as you like.

Being kind means ...

Positive Vibes

**Your positive vibe is contagious.
We are wired to feel other people's
emotions just by looking at them.**

This is down to something called 'Mirror Neurons'
in our brain, which help us to feel empathy.
Scientists[1] studying the brain found that the same
cells light up whether we are 'doing' something
or just 'observing' someone else doing it.

This means our brain is wired to
experience someone else's emotion as though
we were experiencing it ourselves.

What does this mean for you?

It means your emotions are contagious. When you smile
at someone, for example, all sorts of neurons are firing in
your brain. When they see you smile, a few of those same
neurons will fire in their brain, causing them to smile as
well – even if it's just for a split second. Try it! Go out into
the world and spread some joy. Your actions will ripple out
and help to create the kind of world we all want to live in.

Add Kindness to Your To-Do List

When we're too busy, it leaves little room for us to think about others.

There are so many things that can demand our immediate attention and feel urgent. A full inbox, a messy house, those little red notifications on our phone – no matter how many things are on your to-do list today, make sure one of them is something kind for someone else. Even a small act of kindness that helps someone feel more positive or valued has the potential to have a powerful and lasting impact on that person, and on their interactions with others. It will also help you feel happier and calmer.

My To-Do List

....

....

....

....

....

....

....

....

....

'You will never
have a completely bad
day if you show kindness
at least once.'

GREG HENRY QUINN

What Do You Have to Offer?

Every single one of us has something to offer. What are you good at? And how could you use that skill to help someone? Kindness doesn't have to be about giving 'things' and it doesn't need to be a trained skill. Perhaps it is your ability to make people feel relaxed or happy when they are anxious. Your time is precious and devoting a small portion of it to help someone else is worth a lot!

What do you have to offer?

Be All There

Most of us spend almost half of our day thinking about something other than what we're doing.[2]

We go for walk to unwind but think about work
the whole time or spend time with a friend while
worrying about something we said yesterday,
or something that might happen tomorrow.

It means we are rarely fully present and truly
enjoying or embracing the current moment or
giving our full attention to the ones we're with.

Wherever you are today and whatever you're doing, practise making a conscious effort to be 100% there. Use this space to write about or draw what you noticed and how it felt.

'Wherever you go,
go with all
your heart.'

CONFUCIUS

Eye-gazing

Try this little exercise next time you're frustrated with a loved one ... it can help to bring you closer and unlock the kindness and compassion inside you.

You might feel awkward or self-conscious, but it's a powerful technique and can help us to feel more deeply connected (it can work for squabbling children as well!)

Sit comfortably facing one another.

Stare into each other's eyes, without saying a word.
You can blink as much as you like but try not to break
eye contact ... even if it feels silly or uncomfortable.

Do this for two whole minutes.

How did it feel?

....ㅤㅤㅤㅤ..

....ㅤㅤㅤㅤ..

Corona-kindness

When the Covid 19 pandemic hit in
2020, the news was filled with stories of
stockpiling, shortages and fear.

But as the weeks went by, stories of kindness began to
emerge. In times of crisis, there is always kindness. We
came together to stay at home and protect our most
vulnerable. Communities supported one another, families
reconnected and the world slowed down. And when
normal life was stripped away, we were left with what
really mattered … love, family, community and kindness.

There were stories of school children singing their hearts out in playgrounds for the elderly residents nearby, teachers walking miles to make sure vulnerable children still got their lunches, and who can forget Colonel Sir Tom ... the 100-year-old war veteran who walked lengths of his garden to raise a bit of money and became an international hero.

These kindnesses lifted our spirits, stirred our emotions and helped us feel more positive. This is the impact kindness has on us, even when all we are doing is witnessing others being kind.

What kind stories have stayed with you?

'There is no power for change greater than a community discovering what it cares about.'

MARGARET WHEATLEY

Be Kind to Unkind People

Being kind to kind people can feel
quite effortless, but being kind
to someone who is rude?

That takes great strength of character. People who
behave in that way are often the ones who need
kindness the most. Rise above their behaviour
and choose to react from a place of kindness.

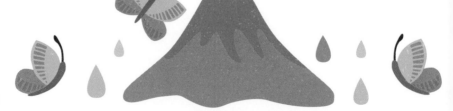

At best, your calm response might encourage
them to be kinder and, at worst, you haven't
let their unkindness rub off on you, which
has shielded your own well-being.

Who do you find it challenging to be kind to?

Why do you think that might be?

....

....

....

....

How could you approach things differently?

....

....

....

....

People's behaviour and choices are always about
them, never about you. What could be going
on in their mind to cause their behaviour?

....

....

....

....

'Why are you so nice, even to people who are rude to you?'

'Because I too have been rude to nice people and I know that rudeness comes from a place of roaring pain, and only kindness soothes it.'

UZMA PARVEEN

Reach Out
and Reconnect

**Who have you lost touch with
but wish you hadn't?**

Take a positive step to rekindle the relationship.
Receiving a kind note, text or phone call
from you could make their day.

People I've lost touch with

How I'm going to reconnect

⬜ text   ⬜ phone call

⬜ email   ⬜ visit

⬜ text   ⬜ phone call

⬜ email   ⬜ visit

⬜ text   ⬜ phone call

⬜ email   ⬜ visit

⬜ text   ⬜ phone call

⬜ email   ⬜ visit

Kindness
=
Happiness

When we're kind to someone,
it doesn't just help that person.
It actually changes our brain chemistry
and helps us to feel happier.

**What are you going to do
this week to be kind?**

Speak to someone who looks lonely

Reach out to a friend

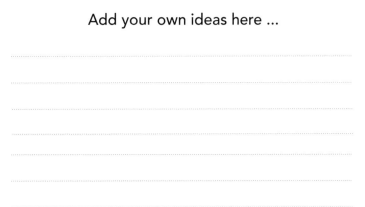

Give someone my full attention

Avoid negative conversations

Add your own ideas here ...

Self-kindness

How you speak to yourself matters. Think about your internal dialogue ... are you kind to yourself or a bit of a bully?

When we think badly about ourselves (and take those thoughts seriously) it can be damaging to our well-being.

When those negative thoughts come into your head,
notice them. Pay attention to how you're speaking to
yourself, because often we do it out of habit, without
even realizing. Just being aware of what you're
doing is a first step to making a positive change.

**Kindness causes elevated levels of dopamine
in the brain, giving us a natural high.**

'Be nice to yourself.
It's hard to be happy when
someone is mean to you
all the time.'

CHRISTINE ARYLO

FOUNDER OF THE INTERNATIONAL
SELF-LOVE MOVEMENT

Forgive Yourself

Do you beat yourself up for past
mistakes? Or for not meeting the
ridiculously high expectations you
set for yourself? It's time to let go.

**What do you give yourself
a hard time about?**

Use this space to address those self-grudges,
then forgive yourself and let it go.

I forgive myself for ...

I forgive myself for ...

I forgive myself for ...

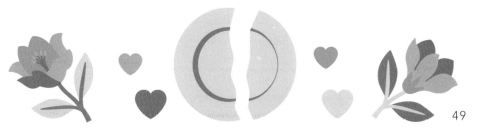

Now Forgive Everyone Else

Holding onto hurt and anger is
stressful, and prolonged stress
is bad for our well-being.

Just as kindness releases hormones that are good for our
bodies, encouraging us to feel happier and more relaxed,
stress releases hormones that put us in 'fight or flight mode',
and negatively affect our physical and mental health.[3]

Is there any anger you're holding onto?

Forgiveness is not just about repairing relationships
– it's about liberating yourself from negative feelings
and moving forward (releasing that chronic stress
and anger will also help you live longer).

Use these pages to get any negative feelings out,
and then make a decision to leave them here, to
close the book and move on. You will feel lighter.

Just. Say. No.

What are you doing out of obligation rather than desire? Have you said yes to something then wished you had said no?

Sometimes the kindest thing we can do for ourselves is just. say. no. It can help you achieve a greater sense of balance, and free you up to say yes to the things that matter most to you.

Things I'm not going to
agree to anymore ...

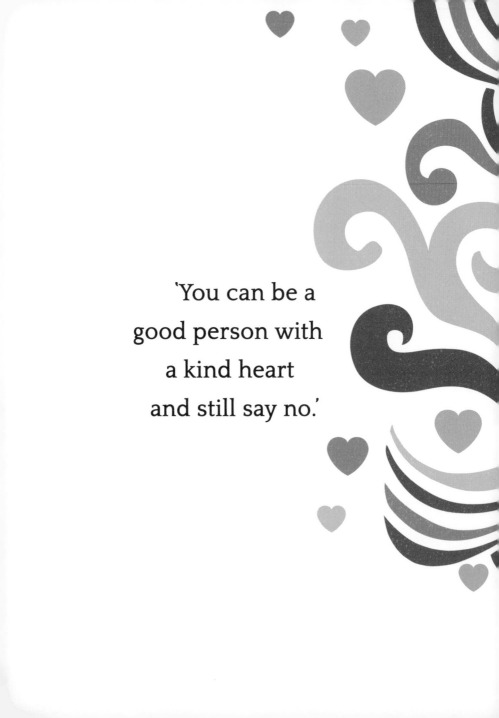

'You can be a
good person with
a kind heart
and still say no.'

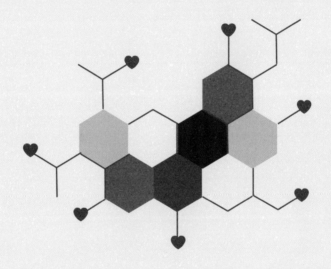

Kindness: the New Botox?

Kindness can actually slow down the ageing process.

Too many free radicals in the body lead to visible
signs of ageing. But being kind produces a hormone called
oxytocin (also known as the 'love hormone'), which
reduces the number of free radicals in our body ...
reducing the formation of wrinkles in the process.

DR DAVID HAMILTON PHD

Conscious Screen-time

Used in a healthy way, technology, our phones, social media ... they're all amazing tools for connecting us and showing kindness.

But on the flipside, they can cause isolation, anxiety[4] and cause us to give less attention to our friends and family. Are there any changes you would like to make with the way you're using technology?

Your choices will soon become your new habits. So make a pledge to use technology in the way that's most beneficial to your well-being ... it could be deciding never to look at a screen while someone is speaking to you, or banning screens first thing in the morning and last thing at night, leaving your phone at home when you go for a walk, or perhaps designating social-media-free weekends. These little habits can be life-changing.

My screen-time pledge ...

....

....

....

....

....

....

....

....

Love Letters

Take a moment to think about the
relationship you have with yourself ... it might
be easier if you imagine it as a friendship.

Is it a toxic friendship that brings you down?

Or is it a friendship filled with
love and acceptance?

When we have a loving relationship with ourselves, it puts us in a better state of mind, which helps us to be kinder, less judgemental and more open-minded.

Take five minutes to write a love letter to yourself. It might feel strange at first but keep going and the words will soon flow. It could be all the things you love about yourself or, if you find that difficult, even just a list of things you feel you're good at or glad about. However you choose to write it, and however long it takes you, make sure these pages are filled with positivity and love.

Come back here to read your own words
whenever you feel in need of a boost.

Give Yourself Calm

People often use meditation as a way to relax or quieten their minds, but did you know it might also help you live longer?

A 'loving-kindness meditation' is one where the focus is on sending compassion, kindness and warmth to ourselves and to others. Research has found that this specific type of meditation could actually slow ageing at a biological level.

If you're new to meditation, start small and build
up slowly. Begin with just a minute or two each
day and gradually add more time each week.

A Simple Loving-Kindness Meditation ...

Find a quiet space, free from distraction, and
sit comfortably. Close your eyes, relax your
muscles and take a few deep breaths.

Imagine feeling nothing but love for yourself. Focus on
this feeling of self-love and imagine that you're breathing
out all your stresses and breathing in feelings of love.

Repeat three or four phrases quietly to yourself. You can create your own or use the simple mantras below. You could also visualize a kind light shining through your body as you repeat the phrases.

May I be well.
May I be happy.
May I be at peace.

Now, send love and kindness to someone else ... think of a good friend or family member perhaps. Bring them to mind as vividly as you can and repeat the same mantra.

May they be well.
May they be happy.
May they be at peace.

Next – if you feel comfortable with this – send love and kindness to someone you have a more challenging relationship with, or someone you dislike. Bring them into your mind and repeat the same mantra.

May they be well.
May they be happy.
May they be at peace.

And finally, send love and
kindness to all beings.

May they be well.
May they be happy.
May they be at peace.

The science bit ...

Researchers at the University of North Carolina[5] found that practicing loving-kindness meditation could slow down biological ageing. Biological ageing can be measured by looking at a section of our DNA called telomeres (as we age our telomere length shortens). Using blood samples, they measured the length of people's telomeres before and after six weeks of daily meditation. They compared people who practiced a loving-kindness meditation, a mindfulness meditation, and a control group who did no meditation at all. They found that people who did the loving-kindness meditation had significantly less shortening of telomeres. Mindfulness meditation also reduced the rate of loss of telomere length, but only a little.

'Feelings of kindness and compassion seem to slow ageing at the genetic level. This offers further evidence that kindness brings about effects that are physiologically opposite to stress, because stress is one of the ways that telomere loss speeds up.'

DR DAVID HAMILTON PHD

Say Sorry...

One little word has the power to heal the
deepest of wounds, rebuild relationships
or even help us feel more connected to
complete strangers. It takes so much strength
and courage to drop our ego and admit our
mistakes, but it only takes a few seconds.

Is there someone you owe an apology to?

'When you forgive,
you free your soul.
When you say sorry,
you free two souls.'

DONALD L. HICKS

See the Good

Sometimes we get stuck in unkind habits,
like gossiping about people. It might seem
harmless, but choosing to see the worst
in people brings out the worst in us.

Being kind, showing compassion, seeing
the good in people and giving them the
benefit of the doubt will earn you trust
and respect, and your positive approach
will benefit your mind, body and soul.

Who do you tend to judge?

....

Is there anyone you speak unkindly about?

....

Why do you think you do this?

....

How do you feel afterwards?

....

'Blowing out someone
else's candles doesn't
make yours shine
any brighter.'

Kindness

=

Less Anxiety

Kindness can actually reduce anxiety.

Researchers from the University of Columbia[6] took a group of highly anxious people and had them perform at least six acts of kindness a week. The results? After one month people who were being kind to others reported feeling more positive and less anxious.

Gratitude > Happiness > Kindness

People who are grateful tend to be happier, and when we feel happier we're more likely to be kind.

Healthier Hearts

Kindness releases the hormone oxytocin. This causes the release of a chemical called nitric oxide which expands our blood vessels, reducing blood pressure and protecting our hearts.

Wherever you are now, look up and pay attention to
all the things that surround you. What are five things
you can see right now that you feel grateful for?

1 ....

2 ....

3 ....

4 ....

5 ....

Live Kindly

Being kind to people creates a better world ... but being kind to the planet will give us a world to live on.

Most of us know what we need to do to live more sustainably but sometimes it's hard to break old habits. If you need some inspiration, here are some little acts of kindness you can do for the planet and some space to add your own.

Buy consciously

Use your purchasing power for good. Try to be more conscious of how much you buy, what you buy, how it's packaged and where you choose to buy it from. These choices matter.

Switch off

Unplug three things in your house right now that are not being used.

Be the change

If you see something you can do to help, do it. Be someone who picks-up the litter, not the person who complains about the litter.

Make a lifetime commitment to a 'bag for life'

How many plastic carrier bags do you have lurking in your house? Fold up a reusable bag and put it in your handbag or car, so you'll always have one to hand when you need it.

Add you own ...

Listening

**How often do you get the chance to speak
without anyone interrupting you?**

Listening – really listening – is a simple
way of showing someone you care. It also
creates space for people to be authentic and
to take the time to explore their feelings.

Try this exercise with a friend
or loved one.

Ask them how they are and then stay silent for two
entire minutes while they speak. You can't say a word
– not even words of encouragement or sympathy.

When the two minutes are up, switch roles.

These moments of silence and quiet exploration can
unlock some of our deepest thoughts and feelings
that we never usually allow ourselves to express.

Thoughts
Are a Bit Like
Teabags ...

If you dip a teabag in boiling water for
a few seconds, what are you left with?
A very weak cup of tea. But if you let it
percolate, stir it around, and constantly dunk
it in and out, it will become stronger.

It's the same with our thoughts. If you have a negative or worrying thought, but don't pay much attention to it, it remains weak and soon passes. But if you hold onto that thought, think about it over and over and let it swirl around in your mind, it becomes stronger and more powerful – to the point where you not only believe it to be true, but feel overwhelmed by it.

Next time you feel overwhelmed or anxious, notice what you have been thinking about. Just being aware that you've been giving too much weight to your negative thoughts can help you understand why you're feeling the way you do. This is a great way to practise kindness towards yourself.

Find the Sunshine

There's a school of thought that says we become more like the people we spend time with.

Positive relationships can bring out the best in us. They not only help us feel better, they can help us be better.

Who do you feel good around?

....

Who brings out your best?

....

What is it about them that helps you feel this way?

....

....

And if you don't feel like you have anyone like that in your
life right now, try to be that person for someone else.

'When you can't find
the sunshine, be
the sunshine.'

The Kindest Thing

What's the kindest thing someone
has ever done for you?

♥

Use this space to write about who it
was, what they did and how you felt.

Why do you think that memory
has stayed with you?

Comparison is the Thief of Joy

If you took someone's most beautiful photos, greatest achievements and most exciting days and compared them with your worst, how do you think you would measure up?

It seems like an unhelpful thing to do, yet it's what many of us do on a daily basis – often subconsciously.

There will always be someone stronger, funnier, wealthier, prettier ... that will never change. What *can* change is our attitude towards that.

Unless you choose to let it, where you are in relation to others has no bearing on your well-being.

3 things I love about myself ...

I am ...

....

I can ...

....

I always ...

....

You're on a roll. Keep them coming.

I am ...

I can ...

I always ...

I am ...

I can ...

I always ...

'A flower does not
think of competing
to the flower next to it.
It just blooms.'

SENSEI OGUI,
ZEN SHIN TALKS

A Kind Story ... The Boy and His Bed

A thirteen-year-old boy called Andy was caring for his mum.

She has disabilities and severe bouts of depression and depended heavily on Andy to look after her.

Andy didn't have a bed and was sleeping on an old mattress on a bare concrete floor in an empty room. The 52 Lives charity heard about Andy and asked people to help. Within days, Andy didn't just have a new bed – he had a whole new bedroom filled with everything he could possibly need. All thanks to the kindness of strangers.

'Never doubt that a small group of thoughtful, committed citizens can change the world®; indeed, it's the only thing that ever has.'

MARGARET MEAD

End Your Day with Kindness

Bedtime is often when we mentally review
our day, which isn't always conducive
to getting a good night's sleep.

Try ending your day with kindness. It
will help to quieten your mind helping
you feel calmer and more content.

Before bed ...

Make a note of three kind things that happened
during your day (it doesn't have to be
something grand ... little things matter)

Three kind things that happened today

1. ....

2. ....

3. ....

Hidden
Battles ...

'Everyone you meet is fighting
a battle you know nothing
about. So be kind. Always.'

I wish people
knew ...

I wish people knew ...

What do you wish people
knew about you?

I wish
people knew ...

I wish people knew ...

Unkindness

We all have unkind moments.

Try to notice what's going on in your mind in those times that you tend to be unkind. Is it when you're trying to do too many things at once and feel overwhelmed? Is it when you're dealing with someone who you find annoying? Is it when someone tells you to get off your phone and the screen-addict in you gets mad? Is it when you're scared? Unkindness is always caused by our state of mind, never from external events. No matter what is going on around us, we always have a choice of how to react.

Are there times when you tend to be unkind?
What is happening in your mind?

Your Top Five

What are the five kindest things you've ever done for someone?

'To give and not expect
return, that is what lies at
the heart of love.'

OSCAR WILDE

Three Ways to be Kind to Yourself

When we look after ourselves, it puts us in a better state to be kind to other people. Here are three little ways you can be kind to yourself today …

Move.

Exercise releases feel-good endorphins, which help to
relieve anxiety and depression. It can also help to take
your mind of any worries and refresh your thinking.

Spend time in nature.

Nature has a way of touching something deep within
us. It gives us a sense of perspective ... of being part
of something much larger than ourselves. Whether
it's a luscious forest or just a few flowers in a pot,
connecting with nature has been shown to help us
feel a greater sense of peace and happiness.

Bedroom ban.

Is your phone the last thing you look at before you go to sleep? Or the first thing you wake up to? Try leaving your phone in another room. Changing the way you start and end your day can make a big difference to your well-being.

Use this space to add your own ...

Create a Daily Kindness Plan

Something I'm going to do
to be kind to my mind today

Something I'm going to do to
be kind to my body today

Something I'm going to do to
be kind to someone else today

More Than an Act ...

We often talk about 'random acts of kindness'
but being kind is about so much more than
performing one-off 'acts of kindness' ...
it's an approach to life. If you think about
kindness in this holistic way, it will touch
every aspect of your day and guide every
choice you make. Let kindness become part
of who you are, not just what you do.

Notes

[1] di Pellegrino, G., Fadiga, L., Fogassi, L. et al. (1992), Understanding motor events: a neurophysiological study. *Exp Brain Res* 91, 176–180

[2] Gilbert, Killingsworth (2010), Harvard University, 'A Wandering Mind Is an Unhappy Mind', *Science*, 330 (6006), 932

[3] Hamilton, David R.: www.drdavidhamilton.com

[4] Melissa G. Hunt, Rachel Marx, Courtney Lipson, Jordyn Young. (2018) 'No More FOMO: Limiting Social Media Decreases Loneliness and Depression'. *Journal of Social and Clinical Psychology*, 751

[5] Khoa D. Le Nguyen, Jue Lin, Sara B. Algoe, Mary M. Brantley, Sumi L. Kim, Jeffrey Brantley, Sharon Salzberg, Barbara L. Fredrickson 'Loving-kindness meditation slows biological aging in novices: Evidence from a 12-week randomized controlled trial', *Psychoneuroendocrinology*, Volume 108, October 2019, Pages 20-27

[6] Jennifer L. Trew, Lynn E. Alden, 'Kindness reduces avoidance goals in socially anxious individuals', *Motivation and Emotion*, 2015; DOI: 10.1007/s11031-015-9499-5